D1519538

Polar Bear Cubs

by Ruth Owen

Consultants:

Suzy Gazlay, M.A.
Recipient, Presidential Award
for Excellence in Science Teaching

Barbara Nielsen
Director of Communications
Polar Bears International

BEARPORT
PUBLISHING

New York, New York

Credits

Cover, © Alaska Stock LLC/Alamy; 4–5, © Tom Soucek/Alamy; 6–7, © Konrad Wothe/Minden Pictures/FLPA; 8–9, © Suzi Eszterhas/Minden Pictures/FLPA; 10–11, © All Canada Photos/ Superstock; 12, © Bruce & Jan Lichtenberger/Superstock; 13, © Matthias Breiter/Minden Pictures/FLPA; 14, © age footstock/Superstock; 15, © Alaska Stock LLC/Alamy; 16–17, © Rob Reijnen/Minden Pictures/FLPA; 18, © Steve Bloom/Steve Bloom Images/Alamy; 19, © ZSSD/Minden Pictures/FLPA; 20, © VikOl/Shutterstock; 21, © Juniors Bildarchiv/Alamy; 22T, © All Canada Photos/Superstock; 22C, © Bruce & Jan Lichtenberger/Superstock; 22B, © Shutterstock; 23T, © Aron Ingi Ólason/Shutterstock; 23B, © VikOl/Shutterstock.

Publisher: Kenn Goin
Editorial Director: Adam Siegel
Creative Director: Spencer Brinker
Design: Alix Wood
Photo Researcher: Ruby Tuesday Books Ltd

Library of Congress Cataloging-in-Publication Data

Owen, Ruth, 1967–
  Polar bear cubs / By Ruth Owen.
    p. cm. — (Wild baby animals)
  Includes bibliographical references and index.
  ISBN-13: 978-1-61772-157-1 (library binding)
  ISBN-10: 1-61772-157-3 (library binding)
  1. Polar bear—Infancy—Juvenile literature. I. Title.
  QL737.C27O96 2011
  599.786'139—dc22

                          2010041247

For more information, write to Bearport Publishing Company, Inc., 101 Fifth Avenue, Suite 6R, New York, New York 10003. Printed in the United States of America in North Mankato, Minnesota.

121510
10810CGC

10 9 8 7 6 5 4 3 2 1

Contents

Meet some polar bear cubs

Two polar bear **cubs** cuddle with their mother.

They are three months old.

Soon the mother bear will begin to teach the cubs how to live on their own.

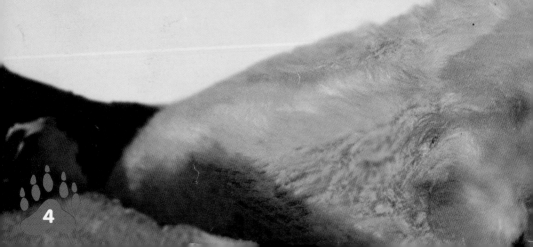

Polar bear mother

Polar bear cubs

5

Where do polar bears live?

Polar bears live near the **North Pole**.

The North Pole is one of the coldest places on **Earth**.

It is so cold that parts of the ocean **freeze**.

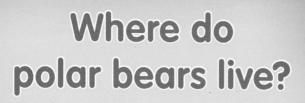

Asia

North Pole

Arctic Ocean

Europe

Africa

Pacific Ocean

North America

Atlantic Ocean

South America

Where polar bears live

How do polar bears keep warm?

Polar bears have thick fur to keep them warm.

They also have a layer of fat under their fur.

This helps keep them warm, too.

Sometimes polar bears get too hot!

They can cool off in the snow.

Thick fur

How big is a polar bear?

Polar bears are huge!

They are nearly as tall as adult humans.

They are the biggest land animals that hunt for food.

A polar bear's **paws** are as big as dinner plates!

Adult polar bear size

Paw

In the den

Near the start of winter, a mother bear digs a tunnel under the snow.

This cozy home is called a **den**.

Den

A mother bear stays in the den all winter.

Her cubs are born in the den.

The mother feeds the cubs milk from her body.

Cub feeding

Leaving the den

By early spring, the bears leave the den.

The cubs are about three months old.

The mother watches for enemies.

The cubs like to play.

15

Going hunting

Polar bears eat seals.

The mother teaches her cubs how to hunt.

She waits by a hole in the ice.

When a seal pops up, she kills it with her teeth and paws.

Seal

Hole in the ice

Mothers and cubs

Polar bears walk for miles looking for seals to eat.

Mothers sometimes carry their cubs if they get tired.

Swimming cub

Polar bears also swim for miles looking for seals to eat.

Mothers teach their cubs how to swim.

Time to leave home

The cubs leave their mother when they are two to three years old.

Each cub will now hunt and live on its own.

The cubs are ready to become grown-up polar bears!

Glossary

cubs (KUHBZ) the babies of some animals, such as bears, lions, and tigers

den (DEN) a home where wild animals can rest, be safe, and have babies

Earth (URTH) the planet on which people live

freeze (FREEZ) when a liquid, such as water, gets so cold that it becomes solid

North Pole
(NORTH POHL)
the northernmost
point on Earth

paws (PAWZ) the feet of an animal that has four feet and claws

Index

Read more

Miller, Sara Swan. *Polar Bears of the Arctic (Brrr! Polar Animals)*. New York: Rosen (2009).

Orme, Helen. *Polar Bears in Danger (Wildlife Survival)*. New York: Bearport (2007).

Sjonger, Rebecca, and Bobbie Kalman. *The Life Cycle of a Polar Bear*. New York: Crabtree (2006).

Squire, Ann O. *Polar Bears (A True Book)*. New York: Children's Press (2007).

Learn more online

To learn more about polar bears, visit **www.bearportpublishing.com/WildBabyAnimals**

About the author

Ruth Owen has been writing children's books for more than ten years. She lives in Cornwall, England, just minutes from the ocean. Ruth loves gardening and caring for her family of llamas.

24